FANTAS

Ruth Kelly

ARTHUR H. STOCKWELL LTD.
Elms Court   Ilfracombe   Devon
Established 1898

British Library Cataloguing-in-Publication Data.
A catalogue record for this book is available
from the British Library.

By the same author:
Cascades of Thought

ISBN 0 7223 3320-X
Printed in Great Britain by
Arthur H. Stockwell Ltd.
Elms Court   Ilfracombe
Devon

Contents

The Magic Carpet

Flying high, up in the sky,
Watching the clouds go rolling by;
Passing the sun, up above
On a magic carpet filled with love.

Still going strong, through the air,
Miles and miles from anywhere;
In wind and rain and all kinds of weather,
A friend and I, are flying together.

Flying high and whistling a tune,
Sweeping the stars and over the moon;
It's a great adventure, as exciting as can be,
Looking down at the deep blue sea.

Soon we will land
Upon the rich and golden sand;
Always there, close at hand,
The magic carpet, to command.

My Childhood Days

Playing rounders in the sun,
As the school holidays,
Have just begun.
On the swings in the park,
Rising early with a lark.

In the valley picking rhubarb, from the greens,
Shaking apples down from the trees.
In the field, watching the goats,
Feeding Dolly the horse,
Her oats.

Having a game of marbles,
With the lads.
Playing hopscotch on the flags;
Catching tadpoles in the lake,
Feeding the pigeons,
Some home-made cake.

Roller skating with Angela and Jean,
Doing handstands on the green;
Blind man's buff was my favourite treat,
Hide-and-seek in the street.
Riding bikes with Ann and Harry,
Playing tennis with Joy and Barry.

Sitting on the embankment,
Waving to the trains as they pass by,
Just like the 'Railway Children',
With my friends,
Margaret, Beryl and I.

A Picnic

A picnic is great fun,
Spreading the tablecloth,
Out in the sun;
Upon the grass so green,
You and I, Mary Jean.

A flask of coffee, piping hot;
Jam tarts, quite a lot.
Chicken legs and lemonade,
Let's sit here in the shade.

Brown bread sandwiches,
Cheese and ham;
Look who's waving, little Sam;
Fancy cakes and jelly tots,
Candy sticks and lollipops.

The sound of traffic,
From the road,
The croaking of a baby toad;
Grasshoppers jumping around our feet,
Waiting for a special treat.

Time to call it a day,
Pack the things and clear away;
Before we have a drop of rain,
We'll visit this spot once again.

The Teddy Bear

The Teddy Bear with furry hair
And glassy eyes, shining bright,
A talking Teddy that says 'good night'.
He's very cuddly to take to bed,
You can call him 'Little Ned'.

Make him a jacket and a cap,
Rock him to sleep on your lap;
Take him for a walk in the wood,
If it starts to rain,
He's got a cape and hood.

There are lots of Teddies, new and old,
Some you keep, some are sold;
He's Ned the playmate with floppy ears,
Cherish him throughout the years.
Welcome Teddies everywhere,
Give them love and show them care.

A Robin

I heard a robin singing
One morning in June,
As I opened the window;
Such a lovely tune.

Sat upon the garden gate,
She's an early bird;
Never late.
Scratching for food on the lawn,
She's been up since dawn.
Made a nest, not very far;
You can hear her chirping,
Wherever you are.

Sitting on her eggs till they hatch out,
Then little chicks begin to sprout;
She perches on a blackberry bush
And calls out loudly to the thrush.

The Circus

Come to the circus
And have a good time;
Watch all the elephants join trunks in a line.
Monkeys doing tricks,
Lions being tamed, just for kicks.
There's the ringmaster,
The animal boss,
Children eating candyfloss.

Brave men eating fire,
A trapeze act,
With a high flyer;
Funny clowns to make you laugh,
A baby elephant taking a bath.

Balloons and sideshows,
By the score;
Get your tickets at the door.

The Wind

The wind blows high,
Sweeping through a cloudy sky;
Windmills blowing round and round,
Standing upright in the ground;
Windows rattling, doors as well,
When it will stop, you never can tell.

Dustbins blowing down the street,
Littered rubbish at your feet;
Whistling down the chimneypots,
Slate crumbling on the rooftops.

Birds twittering in the trees,
They know it's more than just a breeze.
Candles flicker and lights go dim,
The gushing of the wind
That howls within.

A Tree

A tree stands firm and tall,
During autumn the leaves start to fall.
In winter time the tree is bare,
It looks so forlorn
With no one to care.

You may carve your name in the bark,
To you, it's just a lark.
Most people will say it's only a shrub,
Instead of being kind and showing love.

While the weather's hot, it will give you shade,
Till the leaves turn brown and begin to fade.

A fine handsome tree in the sunshine,
Bearing fresh fruits on the vine.
If I spoke to a tree would it listen to me?
I'm sure it wouldn't be mean or disagree.

It could be a friend, a real chum
And never deprive you of a plum.
A tree is God's creation, root and stem,
So always remember not to vandalize them.

The Moon

The moon shines bright on a winter's night,
To guide your way and give you light;
Moonbeams are shining everywhere,
As you walk home without a care.

The moon, a ball of light,
When the sun goes down,
It comes out at night;
Very mellow, with a kind of face,
The man in the moon,
You can never trace.

It's like a broken promise,
Made of green cheese,
As people may say, but it's only a tease;
A blue moon, a new moon,
On a cold night,
Shining with a silvery light.

Hugging the clouds in the dark sky,
Shining down on the passers-by;
A guided light for you tonight,
A harvest moon, big and bright.

The Sun

The sun shines bright on a summer's day,
Peeping through the trees in the month of May.

The sun a ball of fire,
Blazing down with great desire;
Sunbeams are sparkling in the sky,
Gleaming down and dazzling your eye.

Sunshine will make the vegetables grow,
Melt away the ice and snow;
Sun brings happiness all the time,
The moment it begins to shine.

Sun brings heat,
And makes life feel more complete;
It is very pleasant any time of day,
But be careful of its harmful ray.

As the daylight goes out of sight,
The sun's no longer bright;
It retires behind the clouds at night,
And rises again at first light.

The Golden Goose

I wish I had a golden goose,
On a feather bed;
Every time I stroked her head,
She'd lay a golden egg.

The first miracle on the farm,
As the cock crowed,
To sound the alarm;
Weighing the eggs, two by two,
I'd like to think it all came true.

Lots of reporters on the loose,
Taking pictures of the goose;
It's just a fictitious yarn,
Wishful thinking in the barn.

Butterflies

Once a caterpillar on a tree,
Brown and furry, soft as can be;
Then a butterfly overnight,
Their tiny wings, colourful and bright.

Don't try to catch them in a net,
You couldn't keep one as a pet;
Butterflies do no harm to anyone,
Beautiful to look upon;
Landing on the windowpane,
Then flutter gently down the lane.

The Sea

The sea, the wide world ocean;
All ships that sail on her waters so blue,
Are well equipped with a decent crew.
The waves beating on the shore,
Flowing through the Channel
For evermore.

The tide swept in onto the land,
Wetting deck chairs and the sand;
Seashells and pebbles
Washed from afar,
Collected by a child
And placed in a jar.

Crabs and turtles, jelly fish too,
Swimming around out in the blue;
The lighthouse stood so tall,
Way out in the mist, beyond the sea wall.
Glassy calm or rough as can be,
That's the true nature of the sea.

The Clock

The clock hangs on the wall,
Chiming loudly in the hall;
Its lovely mahogany case,
With an illuminous, pretty face.

"Tick tock," went the clock,
As it keeps you company,
On a winter's night,
Giving out the time,
By candlelight.

As the clock strikes nine,
For supper time,
There's bread and cheese
And a glass of wine;
A blazing fire, burning bright,
You can hear the ticking of the clock,
In the still of the night.

The Mermaids

Swimming in the deep blue sea,
There's a number of mermaids as happy as can be,
Floating by to and fro,
Singing softly as they go.

Very attractive, what a dish,
Half a woman and half a fish;
Their tails bobbing up and down,
As they swim along without a frown.

When a mighty storm breaks out,
Run for cover, hear them shout.
The mermaids shelter in the caves,
Where they hide out for days and days.

When things are calm once again,
They return to the rocks and sit so vain,
Watching the ladies having fun on the beach,
Longing to show themselves,
But they are way out of reach.

If mermaids were spotted in the mist,
Would people believe that they really exist?

The Rocking Chair

There's an old rocking chair,
In need of some care,
In an old house,
Covered in dust and mould
And worth a fair penny, if sold.

New tenants moved in,
The house became alive;
The door opened wide
You could see inside,
The old rocking chair,
Shining so bright,
It had been polished overnight.

Rocking about, to and fro,
It seemed to be dancing to the radio;
Friendly people within,
Invited us in for a glass of gin;
As I was leaving, I began to stare,
For still going strong,
Was the old rocking chair.

I wonder how much it would fetch today?
I'd rather not say.
It's well looked after
And handled with care,
But they will never part,
With the old rocking chair.

The Birth of Christ

Mary had a virgin birth,
A miracle from God, a son on Earth;
Sent from heaven up above,
A little king for us to love.

Born in a stable,
A saviour child,
In a manger pure and mild;
Wise men came from afar,
Guided by a shining star,
Bringing gifts of myrrh and gold,
Frankincense the Bible told.

Bells are ringing, children singing,
Telling the news this day;
Jesus Christ, born on Christmas Day.

Monkey Business

There was a ship of America
Sailed out into the blue,
With a cartload of monkeys,
All a joyful crew.

When roared the deep sea gales,
See the happy crowd
Swinging by their tails;
Then all sitting cross-legged
Around a keg of rum,
One playing the trumpet
The other one a drum.

As the ship sailed into land
See the monkeys dash
For nuts across the sand.

The Chimney Sweep

There's a chimney sweep
Down the road,
Like in days of old;
Sweeping chimneys in the street,
Watch the soot fall
At his feet.

The soot can fall very hard,
Make sure you have a fireguard;
It's lucky to have a chimney sweep,
When you get wed.
Or is it an old wives' tale,
We once heard said?

He sweeps the chimneys
Before the night,
So we can have fires
Blazing so bright.

The Cottage

There stood a stone cottage
In a country lane,
With a white picket fence
Made out of cane,
Blooming buds of daffodils
Beneath the fancy windowsills.

So attractive for all to see,
Longing to possess it, and have the key;
I peeped through the window
To see what it was like,
There sat an old gentleman
Smoking a pipe.

Cushion covers, made of lace,
Table mats set in place;
A white napkin beside each plate,
A cosy log fire in the grate.

A nice garden pleasant and gay,
Well looked after everyday.
I'd like to buy that cottage I've seen,
But when I awoke, it was just a dream.

The Snowman

We made a snowman
With a red hat and scarf,
A black pebble nose;
From head to toe,
He was truly froze.

Standing cool
With eyes of coal,
A cute, lonely soul;
Through the window
I could see him clear,
A snowflake on his face,
Like a little tear.

His cherry-lipped mouth,
Had a faint little smile;
He kept me company
For a while,
Until the sun came out one day
And melted him away.

A Wedding Day

A wedding day, that's full of joy,
Later may follow
A girl or a boy.
For richer or poorer
On this happy event,
Saying the vows, that are truly meant;
Bringing the families closer together,
With love and friendship, lasting forever.

So enjoy the years of married life,
A charming husband, and a lovely wife;
May God be with you,
Watch over you,
Bless this marriage
With a love so true.

House Party

At a party, having fun,
As the night has just begun;
Loud music, coming on strong,
People dancing all night long.
A bowl of punch
To spark the night,
Everyone's getting high as a kite;
Bring a bottle on your way in,
You can choose sherry or gin;
There's plenty of tasty food,
Dim the lights, for a party mood.

Waltzing, jiving, doing the Twist,
The music's so lively,
How can they resist!
Drinking and dancing the night away,
Including Frank, Ken and Ray.
Friends and relations
Are starting to yawn,
This party's going on till dawn.

Morning appears very soon,
Make some black coffee,
Don't rattle the spoon;
They've all got a hangover
From the night before,
It's time to go home,
Show them the door.

A Kite

It's every child's delight
To want to fly a kite,
In a wide open space
It will give a good chase.

Just watching a kite
It's a lovely sight,
It's not heavy
But rather light.

Flying high in the sky
Attracting the people passing by;
You will always have fun
When you're flying a kite,
As long as the weather
Is windy and bright.

The Christmas Tree

The Christmas tree stands tall,
Opposite the window, near the wall;
A silver star shining bright,
A tinsel sparkle
As it catches the light.
Fairy lights all a-glow,
Coaches and flowers in a row;
Bells of gold, baubles too,
Displayed on the branches,
A dark shade of blue.

Chocolate money, hung in bags,
Presents wrapped, with little tags;
A snowman with a button nose,
A string of beads, carefully chose;
Crystal lanterns all in white,
Like icicles on a snowy night.

A cherub with a smiling face,
A Christmas candle at the base;
The tree is now fully dressed
Ready for Christmas,
To look its best.

Wild Flowers

You can see the flowers every day,
Growing wild in the fields
Where the children play;
Buttercups, clovers, lupins too,
Still wet with the morning dew;
See the flowers on the grass,
Very pleasant as you pass.

Take a walk and pick a bunch,
To decorate the table
When you're having lunch;
Brighten up the living room,
Watch the buds begin to bloom,
Reminding you of your childhood days;
Hard times in many ways.

Picking flowers, making daisy chains,
Hurrying home before it rains;
Wild flowers entwined around every tree,
As old times still linger in our memory.

The Caravan

A mobile house on wheels,
Where you can have all your meals;
Very handy, within reach,
A few yards from the beach.

Draped curtains on the door,
Pull-out beds, sleeps six or four;
Cups and saucers, plates too,
A bathroom suite in navy blue.

A dining table, and four chairs,
No climbing up flights of stairs;
Running water, faucets of chrome,
A caravan is the ideal home.

A Bicycle for Two

Riding through the countryside,
On a tandem, far and wide;
Our hair blowing in the breeze,
As Sal and I pass by the trees.

The sweet smell of fresh air,
Noise from a nearby fair;
Along the cobblestone lanes,
Avoiding all the cartwheel stains.

Passing by a dried-up well,
With flowery hedges of bluebell;
It's getting late in the afternoon,
Sal and I must ride back soon.

Moody Blues

Cindy married Fred,
Who was ever so mild;
But the tables turned,
When they had their first child.
A beautiful daughter,
A Shirley Temple twin;
Curly hair and dimpled chin.

Cindy felt like she had been put to a test,
Kept her faith, did her best.
A few years later,
Cindy had another child;
Still Fred remained moody and wild.
A child so lovely, with hazel eyes,
Like an angel sent down from the skies.

Cindy a true mother
Straight from the heart,
Gave her children
A brand-new start.

Glad Rags

On the precinct in the town,
Window-shopping up and down;
In and out of all the shops,
Buying lots of coloured tops.

Blouses galore in blue and green,
Fit for a princess or a queen;
A winter cardigan in brown,
Or a satin, evening gown.

A pink coat with a matching muff,
A white fur collar
With a blue trim cuff;
Nylon stockings, ankle strap shoes,
Worn with a pair of silky black trews.
Spend and choose
You just can't lose,
To chase away those winter blues.

A Calendar Expression

January and February, brings the snow,
Makes you tingle from head to toe;
March comes in like a lion,
Roaring winds so strong,
Whistling through the trees
All night long.
The month of April bringing showers,
Watering all the lovely flowers;
Sunny spells in-between,
Men bowling on the green.
Around comes the month of May,
When the lambs are out at play;
A babbling brook murmuring low,
A soft gentle breeze begins to blow.
The bursting out of June,
When all the roses bloom;
Orange blossom in the air,
Blushing brides everywhere.
July and August, summer weather,
Wishing it could last forever;
On holiday in the sun,
Making friends and having fun.
September's here, then October,
Fine and fresh, with trodden clover;
All the summer months are over.
November comes, bringing the fog,
Not a boat on the lake,
Just a floating log.
December month is Christmas time,
Folks are merry, drinking wine;
It's bitter cold but never fear,
For there are twelve months in every year.

Orchard

All kinds of fruit trees
Grown on rich land,
Planted from root
By the gardener's own hand.

Apple trees, pear trees,
There they stand,
Ever so sturdy and grand.

Plums, cherries, as ripe as can be,
Hung in clusters on the tree;
Rosy red apples, firm and round,
Fallen fruit on the ground.

Welcome Home

Welcome home,
I've missed you so,
More than you will ever know.
Glad you're back
Safe and sound,
Celebrating on the ground.
Next time you take a trip away,
Think of me a little each day.

The Black Stallion

The stallion galloped across the moors,
On a windy day, as the rain pours;
His head held high with pride,
The wild stallion that no one can ride.

Many have tried to catch him, but no one can;
He outsmarts any man.
With no warning or sign,
He breaks the ropes every time.

Running free, once again,
The black stallion you can never tame.

The Patched Curtains

I bought a pair of curtains
From a jumble sale;
I noticed a big red patch
As I hung them on the rail.
Everybody laughed,
They thought it was so funny;
Little did they know,
The patch would bring me money.

A friend came over to my house
To have a game of rummy;
Every time I touched the patch,
I was in the money.
I placed a bet on a horse
Named Red Dandy;
The horse came in at ten to one,
I celebrated with the brandy.

I put my money on a dog
Down at the track;
He came first in the race
And I won a stack.
Call it a coincidence
If you may,
Or was it really those curtains
Brought luck my way?

The Train

The train goes speeding along the track
Picking up passengers on the way back,
Waiting on the platform
For the five-past nine,
The stationmaster sees it's on time.

Visiting many lovely places
With all kinds of people
And different faces;
On we go to the next town,
The weather's changed, it's pouring down.

Travelling through the countryside
Under bridges, narrow and wide;
With special memories for you to keep,
As you gaze through the window
At the passing sheep.

Remember the steam trains
From long ago,
When you heard the whistle blow
It gave a warm feeling, and a glow.
But time passes and moves on;
Most trains are electric,
Those days are gone.

Forever Friends

Good friends we have been,
For many years;
Friends are hard to find.
I've enjoyed your company very much,
We will always keep in touch.

You have been a very good friend to me,
The best I ever had;
I am sorry to see you leave,
It makes me very sad.

When you retire
I will miss your smiling face,
For there's no other friend
Can ever take your place.

The Busy Bee

The buzzing of the bee
All day long,
Among the flowers, near the pond;
Settling on a branch
Of the apple tree, so ripe,
With a coat of black
And a yellow stripe.
The busy bee, making honey
So sweet, and good,
Like the freshness of a summer bud.

A Christmas Alphabet

A is for the angel on the Christmas tree.

B is for the bells, ringing merrily.

C is for a Christmas card we all send,
to a very special person, or a dear friend.

D is for the decorations, hanging on the wall.

E is for each child, as God loves them all.

F is for Father Christmas, who brings all the
children's toys.

G is for glad tidings, to all the girls and boys.

H is for the happiness we all help to make.

I is for the icing, on the Christmas cake.

J is for the Lord Jesus lying in a manger.

K is for a king, a welcomed little stranger.

L is for a lantern burning bright.

M is for the mistletoe, where we steal a kiss good
night.

N is for Noel, a Christmas carol so dear.

O is for the organ, playing loud and clear.

P is for the purpose of a Christmas spirited cheer.

Q is for the Queen's speech, she gives every year.

R is for Rudolph the reindeer, with his red nose.

S is for the star that twinkles and glows.

T is for the tender love, we all have to give
and share it with others, as long as we live.

U is for united with all your folks.

V is for the visitors, with all the party jokes.

W is for a Christmas wish, we never tell.

X is for Xmas, we enjoy so well.

Y is for a yulelog, a chocolate roll so sweet.

Z is for a Christmas alphabet, complete.